PET COOKBOOK

EASY EVERYDAY RECIPES FOR HAPPY HEALTHY PETS

Kim McCosker

AUTHOR OF 4 INGREDIENTS
THE INTERNATIONALLY BESTSELLING COOKBOOKS

PET COOKBOOK

4 Ingredients
PO Box 400
Caloundra QLD 4551
+61 7 5341 8282

ABN: **17 435 679 521**

🌐 4ingredients.com.au
f facebook.com/4ingredientspage
▶ 4 ingredients Channel
🐦 @4ingredients
📌 @4ingredients
📷 4 Ingredients
✉ info@4ingredients.com.au

Photography:	**4** Ingredients
Design & Formatting:	Shem Hunter – shemhunterdesign.com
Printing & Binding:	McPhersons Printing Group, Maryborough VIC. Australia
Australian Publisher:	Simon & Schuster AUS
New Zealand Publisher:	Simon & Schuster AUS
ISBN:	978-0-9944478-3-8

Dear Mum and Dad. I
Want a dog really bad. Can I please
have one? It would be ridiculous
not to give me one. ✓

If you do not think I should have
one these are the reasons, I
will take care of it and I will
feed it evry day. I dont mind
If my brother plays with him.
I will pay for it. It is ①
really cute and play full. It
will be incredible If you give me one.
I will pat it and give it lots of
love. I will be alot more quite becus
because
I will be playing with it in my room.

I love dogs Mum and Dad, please
can I have a dog? ✓
from your lonely child Flynn. ✓

A super effort, Flynn!
25/02/17

THERE ARE 4.2 MILLION DOGS IN AUSTRALIA

THERE ARE 3.3 MILLION CATS IN AUSTRALIA

FUR-MAMA

I'm a devoted Mum to three beautiful boys, trying my hardest to raise thoughtful, kind, clever and healthy kids. To do this, my husband and I have surrounded them with pets. Animals that love them, and that they love in return.

We, like 8 million others in Australia, have pets. I'm a Fur-Mama and I truly believe that pets are a lesson in life. They require walks and water, play time and sleep time, love and attention, washing, brushing, shelter and nourishment to give them the best chance at a long, happy and healthy life.

Just as cooking for family and friends is rewarding, so to it is when you cook delicious, healthy, homemade meals for your pets. No additives, no preservatives and no numbers. At home, we know exactly the ingredients that make their meals and nourish them. Home cooked foods are economical and allow us to cater for the different nutritional needs our many varied pets may have. We've had our beautiful Cavoodle, Johnny for over 8 years and he loves chicken jerky, but at $30/kg it's expensive when you compare chicken breast at $9.99/kg and the simplicity of making your own.

It is my hope that the information and recipes within inspire you to cook delicious, nutritious food for your pets. They will absolutely love your efforts, their tail will wag continually, they will purr contentedly, their eyes will glaze with admiration and thanks and just as you feel like "Mother Earth" when you make something your children gobble up, so you will, when your pets do to.

Happy Cooking

Kim

AUTHOR'S DISCLAIMER

I am not a veterinarian, nor a nutritionist, in fact, I did a degree in International Finance at university.

But I write cook books; simple, easy, practical cookbooks and as a family who have had the sweetest dog for 8 years, a Guinea pig for 3 years and three goldfish just about to turn 1. They aren't just our pets; they are our family.

Over the years, our extended family has been varied, chickens, cats and for a brief moment even a mouse. We have forged a great relationship with our vet and, with a good dose of common sense, have managed to raise happy healthy animals. With my boys, we regularly make treats and dinners for our pets and it's only natural to extend these recipes to families looking for homemade alternatives by sharing our 'pet cookbook.'

This is a summary of those simple recipes and should be considered a guide, not gospel.

Use this book logically, if for eg., your dog has allergies or other health issues, if it is a show dog, work dog, or breeding dog then dietary requirements will vary. Please consult your veterinarian with any concerns and enjoy PET COOKBOOK for what it is - a simple, practical guide.

CONTENTS

WHAT TO FEED YOUR PETS

I worked on this book for over a year. Initial research was confusing, as there are many conflicting reports and opinions, one expert telling you something is OK, while the very next tells you why it is wrong. There's a lot of varying opinions when it comes to animal nutrition.

Looking for basic guidelines, I rang the Australian Veterinary Association (AVA) and spoke to their National Marketing Manager who guided me to the World Small Animal Veterinary Association (WSAVA) and their Global Veterinary Development Nutritional Assessment Guidelines. Although this offers no specific advice on which foods to give which animals and is written for veterinarians, it provides good guidelines to assess the nutritional health of your pet.

WSAVA Global Veterinary Development
The WSAVA has developed a global initiative to standardize five vital signs as part of a routine physical check-up and the overall health for all small animals.

These are:
1. Temperature
2. Pulse
3. Respirations
4. Pain assessment
5. Nutrition assessment.

Good nutrition enhances our pets' quality and quantity of life and incorporating it into regular pet care is critical for maintaining their health, as well as their response to disease and injury.

It is imperative to work with a veterinarian to determine if current amounts and types of food are appropriate, based on our pets' life stage, lifestyle and level of activity, disease, body condition and medications.

If diet factors are determined to be inadequate, together, prepare a plan for food and treats that provide appropriate calories and nutrient content for the longest, happiest life possible for our beloved pets.

A PET PARENT'S PANTRY

The following is a list of ingredients in the recipes that comprise this cookbook. **NOTE:** I do not own all of these at any one time, I simply buy them when required, knowing they are not harmful to my pets. Naturally every pet is different, please use as a practical guide, and consult your veterinarian with any concerns.

DOGS

Apple
Bacon, nitrate free
Banana
Beef stock
Boneless fish fillets
Brown rice
Salmon
Cannellini beans
Cottage cheese
Chicken; breast, thigh, mince
Beans
Broccoli
Coconut oil
Carrots
Cheese
Mint
Eggs
Flaxseed, ground
Kale
Kidney beans
Mince
(lean beef, chicken or turkey)
Milk
Natural peanut butter
Natural yoghurt
Rolled oats
Omega 3 or 6 oil
(flaxseed or fish)
Parmesan cheese
Parsley
Pork, mince
Quality dry dog food
Spinach
Sweet potato
Raw honey
Tuna
Wholemeal flour

CATS

Salmon, boneless
Brown rice
Blueberries
Broccoli
Cheddar cheese
Chicken breast
Chicken liver
Chicken stock
Cottage cheese
Eggs
Fish sauce
Green beans
Liver
Natural yoghurt
Mince
(lean beef, chicken or turkey)
Mint
Polenta
Powdered milk
Spinach
Rolled oats
Oil olive / vegetable / cod
Parmesan cheese
Parsley
Sardines, canned in oil
Tuna, canned
Wholemeal flour

GUINEA PIGS

Apple
Asian greens
Broccoli
Capsicum
Carrots
Citrus
Grapes
Grass hay
Green beans
Green leafy vegetables
Cucumber
Raw honey
Kiwi fruit
Olive oil
Rolled oats
Parsley
Quality guinea pig pellets
Sweet potato
Zucchini

BIRDS & CHICKENS

Apple
Banana
Berries
Bird seed
Broccoli
Brown rice
Carrots
Desiccated coconut
Dried figs
Grapes
Green leafy vegetables
Legumes
Natural peanut butter
Nuts, raw
Oranges
Rolled oats
Polenta
Pawpaw
Pumpkin
Quinoa
Raisins
Raw almonds
Sprouts
Sweet potato
Wheatgerm
Wholegrain bread

PET ALLERGIES

Yes allergies in pets do exist, in fact food allergies can appear in animals at any age. A lot of the common offenders are the most common ingredients in both dog and cat foods. This correlation is not a coincidence. While some proteins might be slightly more antigenic than others, many proteins are similar in form and the incidence of allergic reactions are probably associated with the amount of exposure. Just like humans, it can often take some detective work to determine what food is causing an animals allergic reaction. An elimination diet will most probably be used to determine what food a pet is allergic to.

Consider a Limited-Ingredient Diet

The hardest part of determining the right hypoallergenic diet for your pet is figuring out which ingredients are causing the allergic reaction.

It stands to reason that if you:

1. Choose a limited ingredient diet, and
2. Cook at home

You will have an easier time identifying the ingredients that cause a reaction.

If the food you prepare only contains limited ingredients, you can easily conduct food trials with your dog. BUT... If a food has loads of ingredients, it will be almost impossible to identify the allergen; another strong motive to make your pets homemade foods.

ALLERGEN KEY

Should your pet already have an allergy or intolerance, or perhaps be displaying symptoms of, I've created the following KEY and applied it to each recipe within to help identify those that may be more beneficial to pets that suffer from food allergy or intolerances.

 EGG FREE

 LACTOSE FREE

 NUT FREE

 SOY FREE

 FREEZABLE

 GLUTEN FREE

 NO ADDED SUGAR

 RAW

 VEGETARIAN

PLEASE NOTE: In the recipes within we use for eg., Massel's Stocks, Lea & Perrin's Worcestershire Sauce and Ayam's Fish Sauce. At the time of print, each of these products were certified Gluten Free. There are a variety of stocks and sauces available, not all gluten free. It is important to check the ingredients of all the products you buy every time you shop.

PET FACTS

Dog Years to Human Years

SOURCE:
Purina: "Your Dog's Age in Human Years" and "Caring For Your Dog"
National Pet Wellness Month: "Pet Age Calculator" and "Pet Aging Chart"

Age of Dog	Small Dog (up to 9kg) in Human Years	Medium Dog (9-22kg) in Human Years	Large Dog (22kg +) in Human Years
1	15	15	15
2	24	24	24
3	28	28	28
4	32	32	32
5	36	36	36
6	40	42	45
7	44	47	50
8	48	51	55
9	52	56	61
10	56	60	66
11	60	65	72
12	64	69	77
13	68	74	82
14	72	78	88
15	76	83	93
16	80	87	120

Cat Years to Human Years

There's no reliable scientific way to calculate the relationship between human and cat years. It is generally agreed that the first two years of a cat's life are roughly equal to the first 25 of a human's, and after this, each additional year is around four 'cat years'. Naturally, a cat's life expectancy will depend on many variables such as breed, nutrition and exercise.

World Animal Day

Is celebrated annually on October 4. It is a significant date in the Christian calendar as the feast of St Francis, the patron saint of animals. World Animal Day started in 1931 to highlight the plight of endangered species. The AVA (Australia's peak veterinary body) says "World Animal Day is set aside to celebrate the importance of animals, whether they're our pets, a working dog or just providing a source of wonder in the wild." Perhaps use this date as a reminder to book an annual health check, to keep our furry friends in mint condition.

So many beautiful stories about the Power of Pets, here is but one:

My husband was diagnosed with lung cancer in August 2016 after 6 months of being told he had a fungal infection.

The shock to the family and friends I cannot begin to explain.

Tony went to see the oncology specialist on the Thursday and started chemo on the Friday. The chemo knocked Tony around so much he was in hospital more than he was at home.

Christmas 2016 Tony was in hospital and he had lost so much weight so they gave him another scan only to find out the chemo he was on, was not doing the job and he would only have 3-6 months to live.

The councillor came around to have a talk with Tony and I and asked if we had any children at home or any pets? I said we had 17 year-old twins going into year 12 and that we had no animals. She advised that a puppy would be very good for Tony and the family. So in March we went looking for a dog and found a Cavoodle. Since bringing the dog home (whom we named Maui) my husband's life has improved and been so great. Tony has now been putting on weight and walking with the dog.

The specialist cannot believe how well Tony looks and attributes this improvement in part to little Maui.

WHAT TO FEED YOUR DOG

Unfortunately, there is no easy way to figure out exactly how much individual dogs should be eating. Determining the correct size for meals depends on the type of food dogs are fed, how many times a day they eat, their size, their metabolic rate, the amount of exercise they get and so forth.

As a guideline, I found the below table on petmd.com which is the world's largest digital resource for pet health and wellness information.

Dog's Weight	Amount / Day
2.3kg	½ – ¾ cup
4.5kg	¾ – 1 cup
10kg	1¼ – 1¾ cups
20kg	2½ – 3½ cups
30kg	3½ – 4 cups
40kg	3¾ – 5 cups
45kg	4¼ – 6 cups

These weights and portions are intended as a **guide only** as to what you feed your dog over a 24 hour period. Most adult dogs benefit from eating two meals a day (puppies often require three or more feedings), so you may need to divide the amount by the number of meals you are offering.

Combine this information with the knowledge of your dog's lifestyle to develop your own suitable guide.

DOG ADOPTION

They're loyal, entertaining, caring and their unconditional love is just divine. Across Australia alone, the canine population is estimated at 4.8 million, with 52% of all owned dogs pure bred. And although the Labrador Retriever is the number one dog breed in Australia, there's a few smaller canine breeds becoming more and more popular.

If you are thinking of adding "man's best friend" to your family, remember RSPCA run a fabulous "Adopt-A-Pet" program (www.rspca.org.au/adopt-pet) the site is updated daily and allows you to search for pets available for re-homing in your local area. Adopting a dog is a great way to give a dog or puppy a second chance by providing a loving **fur-ever** home.

We got our beautiful Cavoodle from a home that was downsizing, at the time we thought we were saving him. Turns out, he ended up saving us. We are truly blessed to have a dog that has bought so much unconditional love and joy to our crazy, busy home.

If you are thinking of adding a dog to your family, here is a list of the most popular dog breeds in Australia, 2017 according to Dogs NSW and the Australian National Kennel Council.

1. Labrador Retriever
2. Staffordshire Bull Terrier
3. French Bulldog
4. German Shepherd Dog
5. Border Collie
6. Golden Retriever
7. Cavalier King Charles Spaniel
8. American Staffordshire Bull Terrier
9. Schnauzer (Miniature)
10. Rottweiler

It's not on the list but **RESCUED** is my personal favourite breed!

THE GREATEST GIFT YOU CAN GIVE YOUR PET IS LOVE.

JUST LOVE 'EM!

Steve Irwin

MUTTLOAF

SERVES 8

VEGETABLES: Dogs like veggies and a commonly followed ratio of meat, raw bones and veggies is 50:25:25. Green leafy veggies are vitamin powerhouses, full of antioxidants and minerals. Zucchini, celery, green beans, green peas, red beets, sweet potatoes and other carbohydrate-rich vegetables are all favourites too. In fact, nearly any vegetable mix is fine, so long as it doesn't include onions and is easily digestible.

600g turkey mince

1 cup rolled oats, cooked

¾ cup ground flaxseed

2 eggs

2 cups frozen vegetables, thawed

2 boiled eggs, peeled

Preheat the oven to 180°C.

Line a loaf tin with baking paper.

In a large bowl, mix all the ingredients (except the boiled eggs) together.

Spoon ¼ of the mixture into the loaf tin, enough to cover the base of the tin.

Add the whole boiled eggs, then completely coat the remainder of the mixture.

Bake for 45 minutes.

Stand for 5 minutes before slicing to serve to the absolute delight of your dog. Honestly, Muttloaf is gonna be popular!

ALL-NATURAL DOGGIE CHEWS

MAKES 16

SWEET POTATO: Is a super food, it is rich in an antioxidant called betacarotene,
contains a wide variety of vitamins and minerals and is high in dietary fibre.
You will be surprised how much your puppy will love these easy, economical chews
and how they help keep their teeth nice and clean.

1 large sweet potato, skin on

Preheat oven to 120°C.

Line a baking tray with baking paper.

Scrub the sweet potato, there is no need to peel.

Using a sharp knife, cut it into thin slices (the thinner the slice the shorter the cooking time) and place on the baking tray in a single layer.

Bake for 3 hours, turning half way through.

Cool on a wire rack and store in a dry, sealed container.

Slow baking sweet potatoes is a healthier choice than boiling them, as boiling can cause water soluble nutrients to be lost.

CANINE COOKIES

MAKES 20

CHEESE: Is a great treat for a dog as long as they aren't lactose intolerant, which a small percentage are. Make sure to monitor your dog's reaction and don't overfeed, as many cheeses can be high in fat. If concerned discuss the use of a low-fat cheese in your dog's diet with your vet.

200g beef liver, cooked and chopped

2 kale leaves, thick stems and ribs removed, leaves chopped

½ cup shredded cheese

½ cup milk

1 cup wholemeal flour

Preheat oven to 180°C and line a baking tray with baking paper.

Place all ingredients into a food processor and blend until mixture resembles firm dough.

On a clean, dry surface, roll the dough into a log.

Wrap it in cling wrap and freeze for 20 minutes (this makes it easier to slice).

Remove and slice into 1cm rounds.

Place on a baking tray and bake for 12 to 15 minutes.

Remove from oven and sit for 10 minutes, until dry and crunchy.

Store in an air-tight container in the fridge or freezer until required.

CHICKEN JERKY

MAKES 16

JERKY: Every dog we have ever met loves these. Perhaps because the flavour is concentrated and the jerky chewy and delicious. I love them because they are much cheaper than many commercial varieties, easy to make at home and will keep in the fridge for 2 to 3 weeks in an air-tight container. This jerky is an excellent training dog treat as most dogs will be more than happy to follow directions for this healthy morsel.

2 boneless, skinless
chicken breasts

Preheat the oven to 120°C.

Line a baking tray with baking paper.

Using a sharp knife, slice the chicken breast lengthways, into thin strips.

For hard and dry jerky slice in ½cm strips, for soft and chewy jerky into 1cm strips.

Place the strips on the prepared tray, and bake for 2 hours.

Check the chicken before removing from the oven.

Allow the chicken to cool completely before feeding.

CHICKEN CHOW

SERVES 12

BROWN RICE: Grains such as oats and rice are good choices to include in your dog's diet, especially if you are new to homemade dog food. Both grains are easily digestible carbohydrates which make for a good source of energy if your puppy has an upset tummy or is an older dog. All dogs are individuals, and many do better without grains at all. It's always a good idea to do a poop patrol to see what's getting digested; if you see whole rice in your dog's faeces, he is not gaining the nutritional benefits so there is no point in feeding it.

1.5kg minced chicken meat

2½ cups mixed frozen vegetable (no garlic or onions) minced

4 cups brown rice

Place chicken, vegetables and rice into a large saucepan.

Stir in 6 cups of water until the mixture is smooth.

Place over medium-high heat and bring to a boil, stirring constantly.

Reduce heat to medium-low, cover, and simmer until the rice is tender and all of the liquid has been absorbed, about 25 minutes.

Cool completely before serving; store covered in the refrigerator or freeze into individual serves.

I use brown rice for my entire family, of which my Cavoodle is part of; brown rice is a little higher in protein and a little lower in fat when compared to white rice.

GRANDMA'S GOODNESS

SERVES 4

FISH: Is an easily digestible protein source for dogs and especially those with digestive upsets or with liver or kidney disease. In fact, fish has many advantages, but the main one is its ability to impart so many good vitamins and healthy properties without the increased risk of weight gain (fish is low in saturated fats and calories) or a protein overload causing your dog's internal organs to have to work harder to process the food.

425g tin tuna in oil, drained
1 small carrot, grated
100g sweet potato, grated
1 cup cooked brown rice

In a large non-stick frying pan, toss the tuna to warm through, 2 minutes.

Add the grated carrot and sweet potato, cook for a further 2 minutes, tossing occasionally.

Mix with rice, cook, stirring to warm through.

Cool before serving.

Sprinkle with a little parsley if you have it.

HEALTHY DOGGIE BICKIES

MAKES 24

FLAXSEEDS: Are rich in omega-3 fatty acids, anti-oxidants, nutrients, minerals and vitamins that are essential for optimal health. Flaxseeds also help pass toxins out of our bodies and (ground or oil) are fantastic for a dog's skin, coat softness and shine and can help alleviate itchy skin.

---

1 cup hot water	Preheat oven 180°C and line a baking tray with baking paper.
1 tsp. beef stock	Dissolve the stock in the water.
2½ cups wholemeal flour	In a large bowl, place the flour, flaxseed meal and turmeric.
½ cup ground flaxseed (flaxseed meal)	Add the stock, peanut butter and egg and mix until the mixture forms a large ball of dough.
1 tbsp. turmeric	Onto a clean, floured surface roll out the dough, 1 to 2cm thickness.
½ cup natural peanut butter	Cut and place the shapes onto the prepared tray.
1 egg, beaten	Bake for 20 to 25 minutes.
	For a crispier treat, leave the bickies cooling in the oven for a couple of hours; they become crunchier as they cool.
	Store in an air-tight container for up to 7 days.

HOUND PATTIES

MAKES 6

BURGERS: Whether beef, turkey, salmon or veggie, everyone loves some version of a burger. That includes canines too, who are often found gazing longingly at their owners' burger-filled hands. For the best burgers, choose lean cuts, as too much fat can cause indigestion, acid reflux and other problems. Remember if offering a new food, offer a tiny amount at first, and with burgers, skip the onions, as they're toxic to dogs.

Ingredients	Method
1 cup cooked brown rice	Place all the ingredients in a large mixing bowl.
500g lean beef mince	Mix until well combined.
2 tbsp. finely chopped fresh mint	Shape into 6 large even-sized patties, or 8 medium, depending on the size and appetite of your dog.
	In a non-stick frying pan, cook the patties for at least 4 minutes before turning.
	Cook for another 3 minutes or until both sides are browned.
	Let the burgers rest for 5 minutes before serving.
	If you don't require all at once, place leftover patties in a single layer in a freezer bag and freeze immediately.
	Thaw as needed.

K-9 CUPCAKES

SERVES 12

CAN DOGS EAT CAKE?
The repercussions of dogs eating cake are the same as the repercussions of humans eating cake.
But a little cake on a special occasion is unlikely to hurt a dog – it's simply – A TREAT!

½ cup rolled oats

2 cups self-raising wholemeal flour

¼ cup apple sauce
(or one stewed apple)

¼ cup raw honey

¼ cup natural peanut butter

1 egg

Preheat oven to 180°C.

Line a 12-cup cupcake tray with papers.

In a large bowl, place all the ingredients.

Mix until just combined.

Spoon the mixture evenly across the cupcake tray.

Bake for 15 to 20 minutes.

Cool completely.

Serve as is, or top with a delicious **Doggy Icing** made from whipping together ½ cup natural peanut butter and ½ cup cream cheese with 1 tbsp. honey and a little star made from short-crust pastry. We also used kibble to decorate. Believe me, many are tempted to try these, maybe some of us even did!

LICK 'EMS

MAKES 15

YOGHURT: If you are going to feed your dog yoghurt, make sure he or she is not lactose intolerant and when choosing, pick one that has live active bacteria and no added sugars or artificial sweeteners (aspartame and sucralose can pose mild side effects to your dog, such as an upset tummy, while xylitol has toxic consequences if consumed by a dog). Active bacteria may act as probiotics and, just as they are in humans, probiotics are good for the gut flora of our dogs.

---

2 cups natural yoghurt

1 tbsp. natural peanut butter

2 small ripe bananas, peeled and roughly chopped

Blend all ingredients together into a puree.

Pour into ice cube trays or icy pole moulds and freeze until firm.

Can be kept in freezer for up to two weeks.

Not only will your doggie 'lick em' so will your entire family; my little nephew absolutely loves them, on the day of the photoshoot he ate two!

LEFTOVER LOAF

SERVES 8

LEFTOVERS: Dogs are able to eat a wide variety of food, but know that dogs' digestive systems vary as much as humans, so ease into this slowly, carefully observing how they react to various foods. Giving your dog leftovers on the odd occasion and in small amounts should be okay. Letting them lick the plate or eat the scraps should also be okay as long as you don't give them something that can poison them or damage their digestive system e.g. chocolate, grapes, raisins and onions. I often use leftover vegetables or grains (brown rice or quinoa instead of oats) in this lovely loaf, they just make it go a little further.

600g lean beef mince

2 eggs

1½ cups rolled oats

1 cup grated mixed vegetables
(zucchini, broccoli, carrots
or sweet potato)

½ cup cottage cheese

Preheat oven to 180°C.

Line a loaf tin with baking paper.

Mix all ingredients until well combined, then press into the prepared tin.

Bake for 45 minutes.

Cool before slicing.

Refrigerate or freeze until needed.

For the photo, we served drizzled with gravy and dotted with kibble and peas.

PEANUT BUTTER PUP TREATS

MAKES 24

PEANUT BUTTER: Is a favourite for many dogs. Not only is it a good source of protein but it also contains heart healthy fats and vitamins. Choose natural peanut butter for your dogs (and your children!) and preferably, one without added sugars and other additives. Similarly, bananas are a great treat and very few dogs are allergic to them. In fact, nearly all dogs can enjoy bananas especially performance or working dogs because they contain natural sugars which metabolize quickly providing instant energy.

Ingredients	Method
2 cups rolled oats	Preheat oven to 180°C.
2 ripe bananas, mashed	Line a tray with baking paper.
¼ cup natural peanut butter	In a large bowl, combine oats, bananas, peanut butter and coconut oil.
¼ cup coconut oil	Add an additional 2 tablespoons oats, or until the dough is no longer sticky.
	Working on a lightly floured surface, knead the dough 3 to 4 times until it comes together.
	Using a rolling pin, roll the dough 1cm thick.
	Then with cookie cutters, cut the desired shapes and place onto the prepared tray.
	Bake until the edges are golden brown, about 12 to 15 minutes.
	Cool completely.

MEX 4 REX

SERVES 12

MEX: For Rex, George, Fido, Johnny, Bailey, Buddy, whatever your dog is called, he or she will LOVE this bowl of nutritious colour. The positive impact of proper nutrition on health and disease is well established in all animals. A balanced diet will go a long way to ensuring you have a happy, healthy dog; so take the time to discover what dog food and what quantities are right for your pet.

1kg lean minced beef

1½ cups brown rice

1½ cups kidney beans, drained and rinsed

1½ cups chopped sweet potato

1½ cups chopped carrots

½ cup corn kernels

Place all the ingredients into a slow cooker.

Add 4 cups of water and stir to combine.

Cover and cook on LOW for 5 to 6 hours or HIGH for 2 to 3 hours.

Stir as needed and cool to room temperature.

Store in air-tight containers or zip-lock bags and freeze until required.

MINTIES

MAKES 24

WHEAT: Dogs don't need flour. A dog's ideal diet should consist of meats, vegetables, fruits and other whole foods, however flour presents in many recipes and products. So if you're including flour in your dog's diet, it's helpful to know which ones are the healthiest. Look for wholemeal (or whole grain) flour, wholemeal flours use the entire grain, and therefore contain all the original nutrients.

If you're incorporating flour into your dog's diet, do so gradually. This lets him or her adjust to the new food, and gives you a chance to monitor him to make sure the new flour agrees with his body and taste buds.

¾ cup milk

1 egg

1 cup natural peanut butter

2½ cups wholemeal flour

2 tbsp. freshly chopped mint

Preheat oven 180°C.

Line a baking tray with baking paper.

In a bowl, whisk the milk, one egg and peanut butter.

Add the flour and mint and knead to create a lovely dough; adding mint offers a light and soothing smell to your dog's breath.

With damp hands, gently roll a teaspoon of dough into a ball and place on the prepared tray.

Bake 15 to 20 minutes or until just golden.

Remove and cool.

MUTTBALLS

MAKES 24

Love your dog enough to feed them well.

The next time you see any mince on sale, buy extra as these are drooooly-icious.
In fact, I believe you can make nearly every living dog on the planet happy with our MUTTBALLS!

500g lean sausage mince

2 cups dry dog food
(kibble or biscuits)

¼ cup honey

½ cup grated apple

2 tbsp. Omega 3 or 6 oil
(available from pet stores)

3 tsp. freshly chopped parsley

In a large bowl, mix all the ingredients together (except the parsley) and shape into small, even-sized Muttballs.

Place on a tray and chill for 30 minutes.

Roll in parsley.

Serve fresh or freeze in portions and defrost as needed.

PORKY PEAS

SERVES 8

MINCE: The basis of your dog's diet should be a mix of premium dog food, natural foods including fresh human-grade raw meat and fresh, raw vegetables. I often buy lean mince when on sale or in bulk, and add any number of veggies to make a classic MUTTLOAF, burger patties, rissoles, Mex 4 Rex and the ever popular MUTTBALLS and Porky Peas.

100g lean bacon, diced	In a large non-stick frying pan, sauté the bacon over a medium heat for 2 minutes.
500g pork mince	Add the pork mince and peas along with ¼ cup water.
200g frozen peas, defrosted	Cook until the mince is browned, stirring occasionally.
1 cup cooked brown rice	Cool slightly before mixing through the rice.
	Serve immediately or store in the refrigerator for up to 3 days.

PUPCAKES

MAKES 12

EGGS: Adding eggs to your dog's food is a healthy treat and a fabulous source of very digestible protein and various vitamins and minerals. Eggs are generally safe and nutritious for canine consumption when they're prepared appropriately and fed in limited quantities. An ex-neighbour of mine used to give her German Shepherd his food with crushed egg shell in it. The shell provides almost the same nutrients as bones and are a lot easier to chew especially for aging dogs that cannot chew on bones anymore.

½ cup natural peanut butter

½ cup mashed banana

2 eggs

¾ cup self-raising wholemeal flour

¼ cup rolled oats

½ cup water

Preheat oven to 180°C.

Line a 12-cup mini-muffin tray with papers.

In a large bowl combine the peanut butter, banana and eggs.
Beat together by hand or electric mixer if preferred.

Add the flour, oats and water.

Stir until just combined.

Spoon the mixture across the tray.

Bake for 6 to 8 minutes, or until a toothpick inserted
in the middle of a cupcake comes out clean.

Let cool for a few minutes before moving to wire racks to cool completely.

To make a yummy icing whip 200g cream cheese until soft and light.

Pipe onto the cupcakes and serve topped with gorgeous little heart
made from baked shortcrust pastry.

SALMON LOG

SERVES 12

YUM YUM: Honestly, this Salmon Log is scrumptious. Not only will your fur babies love it,
but simply replace the stock with curry powder, follow the recipe verbatim and
you've got a delightful hors d'oeuvre, served with whole grain crackers, at any event.

425g can salmon	In a large bowl, drain and flake the salmon, discarding any bones.
150g cream cheese	Add the cream cheese and stock and mix well to combine.
½ tsp. beef stock	Place a 30cm long piece of baking paper on a flat, clean surface.
½ cup finely chopped walnuts	Spoon the salmon mixture onto it.
2 tbsp. freshly chopped parsley	Lift the paper and roll the mixture to form a log.
	Unwrap and sprinkle with walnuts and parsley.
	Chill for 15 minutes before slicing into 12 rounds.
	Store in a sealed container in the refrigerator for 4 to 5 days.

SUPERFOOD BOWL

SERVES 4

SUPERFOODS: Are foods that are naturally nutrient-rich and therefore especially beneficial for our dog's health. Some of these include; apples, bananas, eggs, sardines and salmon. Salmon is a fatty fish which is also a good source of omega-3 fatty acids. These fats support the immune system and can be beneficial for our dog's skin and coat health. Just make sure it's cooked before serving.

200g cooked salmon
(tinned pink salmon is fine)
½ cup chopped spinach
⅓ cup natural yoghurt
1 cup cooked sweet potato

In a large bowl stir all ingredients together until well combined.

Portion into 4 equal serves.

Store in a refrigerator for up to 4 days.

VEGGIE TREATS

MAKES 16

PEOPLE FOOD: Dogs always seem to be hungry, and love people food. So when looking for a healthy treat to add to your dog's diet, try the vegetables known to be safe for dogs. Not only are they full of vitamins and minerals, but generally they are also low in calories and fat and provide fibre that promotes healthy digestion. As with all foods, portion size is important. Keep your dog's veggie treats small and talk to your vet about adjusting their food intake if you are supplementing your dog's diet with veggies.

Ingredients	Method
1 cup freshly chopped kale	Preheat oven to 180°C.
2 tbsp. freshly chopped parsley	Line a baking tray with baking paper.
1 carrot, grated	In a large bowl, combine kale, parsley, carrots, cheese and oil and mix well.
¼ cup grated cheddar cheese	Add the flour and flaxseed meal.
2 tbsp. olive oil	Gradually add the water, mixing well to make a dough (add more if needed).
2½ cups wholemeal flour	Knead for 1 minute, then roll out to 1cm thickness.
2 tbsp. flaxseed meal	Using a cookie cutter, cut and transfer to the prepared tray.
½ cup water	Re-roll the scraps and continue until the dough is gone.
	Bake for 20 to 30 minutes on the middle rack or until golden.
	Remove; the biscuits will harden more as they cool.
	Store in an airtight container.

WATERMELON PUPSICLES

WATERMELON: Everybody loves watermelon, even dogs (just remember to remove seeds and discard rind). Watermelon is a health-food powerhouse, low in calories, packed with nutrients and at 92% water, is great for hydration on a hot day. Throughout spring and summer we make batches of these; 'popsicles' for us and 'pupsicles' for our fur baby.

1 kg watermelon	Scoop out the melon, discard the seeds and rind.
270g can coconut milk	Blend together with the coconut milk (add more melon if you prefer a darker pink).
	Pour into an ice cube tray and freeze for at least 4 hours.
	THAT'S IT!

NATURAL WAYS TO ENCOURAGE A SHINY COAT

In The Australian 24 April, 2017 there was an article "Australians are spending $12 billion a year on their pets." Naturally, it caught my eye. It went on to say "there are an estimated eight million pet owners, primarily of cats 3.3 million and dogs 4.2 million, which means Australia has one of the highest domestic animal ownership rates in the world."

Pet grooming (in particular, for dogs) is a huge business, and although many owners pay to have a monthly 'clip' here are some other things you can do to encourage 'man's best friend' to shine.

Bathe regularly, but not too much: How often depends on your dog, the length of the coat, and how dirty he or she gets. Bathing once a month is a good general guideline — often enough to keep the coat clean, but not so often that you're stripping the coat of essential oils. There are many varieties, but try to choose a gentle, medicated, pet-friendly shampoo.

Brush regularly: Regular brushing stimulates the skin and hair follicles, which increases the natural production of skin oils that make the coat shiny. Brush your dog at least once every other day.

A little oil: Stir one teaspoon of coconut oil (flaxseed, olive and sunflower will also work) just don't give them too much, that can lead to diarrhoea. Coconut oil may also help clear up skin conditions.

Natural Repellent: Did you know that many ingredients in your garden act as all-natural flea repellent? Steep lemon juice, witch hazel, water, and lavender together to make a simple spray that will help keep your pet flea-free and smelling fresh. FYI: Witch Hazel can be used in some pretty surprising ways, it's an amazing product, I bought a small bottle from Chemist Warehouse.

Protection: Dogs who have no shelter from the elements and are kept outside most days will have coats that change to be more thick and dry simply to provide natural protection. You can just let it be for the colder winter months, or provide additional shelter to encourage a shinier coat.

Oatmeal Bath: Dogs with dull coats often have skin problems, as well. An oatmeal bath helps sooth the skin, tame itching, and leaves the coat soft and shiny. Oatmeal contains Vitamin E, so it works as a natural softener. Simply grind 1 cup rolled oats into a fine powder, fill a tub with lukewarm water, add the powder and stir in until the water appears cloudy, then place your dog in the bath. Pour water on its back and head, avoiding the eyes, and massage for 10-15 minutes. Rinse and pat dry.

Tuna, sardines, and salmon: These are full of healthy omega-3 fatty acids that help contribute to a healthy coat, plus they're delicious to a dog.

CAT FOOD

Cats are **obligate (true) carnivores** which means that they need a source of animal protein to survive. In the wild, cats eat the carcases of the prey animals they catch which consist of raw meat, raw bones, organs, other tissue and digested vegetable matter.

The Australasia Burmese Cat Society website says "Kittens need feeding 4 times a day until about 16 weeks of age reducing to 3 meals a day until about 9 to 12 months when they should be fed 2 meals a day for the rest of their lives." However, rspca.org.au suggests many adult cats tend to prefer several smaller meals throughout the day and night. Offer food 3 to 4 times per day (eating smaller frequent meals has been associated with greater urinary tract health) and fresh, clean drinking water every day. Meals should be varied eg. premium commercial food, tinned food, dry food, raw meat, cooked chicken, and any leftover roast meat. An egg yolk once or twice a week is beneficial. Fresh water must always be available.

According to RSPCA the list of foods you **should not feed your cat** is onions, onion powder, garlic, chocolate, coffee or caffeine products, mouldy or spoiled foods or compost, bread dough, yeast dough, avocado, grapes, raisins, sultanas, raisins, nuts, fruit stones (seeds), corncobs, tomatoes, mushrooms, cooked bones, small pieces of raw bone or fatty foods or trimmings and salt. Also ensure your cat does not have access to string wrappings around rolled roasts or absorbent pads found under meat when wrapped on trays.

A good rule of thumb, is that human food should not make up more than 15% of a cat's diet.

As with many recipes in this book, they are an occasional treat, a guide only to help you find the optimum diet for your **purr-y** friend.

Always check with your veterinarian before introducing new food into your cat's diet or if you have any dietary concerns. Let's do our best to avoid any **cat-astrophes!**

CAT ADOPTION

Cats make wonderful pets. They're affectionate yet independent, and because they don't need a daily walk, they're a manageable option for families on the go. According to Petbarn PTY LTD (who run Petbarn's Adoption Services, a wonderful service making it super easy to bring home a new family member) the most popular cats in Australia are:

Abyssinian

Originally from Ethiopia, the Abyssinian was introduced to Britain around 1868. Their coat is close-lying to the skin with bands of colour along each hair, creating a distinctive pattern referred to as 'ticking'. They have dark-rimmed, expressive eyes of amber, green or hazel, a long slender body, wedge-shaped head and large ears with a tuft of hair at the top.

Loyal and loving cats, they attach themselves to their human and command affection. They enjoy being the centre of attention and are active and noisy. They're intelligent and curious pets with a particular love of climbing. They're also highly social, so expect Bruno, your dog and Molly your Abyssinian to be best friends.

Australian Mist

Perfect for those who live near the bush and have children, an Australian Mist is a sweet, loving and affectionate cat, specially-bred in Australia to be gentle with little ones and native wildlife. They have a short, dense coat with multi-coloured dark spots on a light, 'misted' beige background.

Super affectionate, they love playing games with their humans and, while trainable, often remain kitten-like for life. Highly tolerant of handling and not inclined to scratch, they thrive on human interaction and love to nestle in laps.

Persian

Hailing from Turkey and Iran, regal Persian's have a luxurious, long coat, enjoy spending their days grooming themselves and sitting prettily somewhere they can be admired.

They have a calm, sweet temperament and are not overly active, which makes them perfect for quiet households. While generally placid, at times they'll have short bursts of kitten-like energy before falling asleep in the sunniest corner of the room. Keep a vacuum cleaner handy, as they're known to shed heavily.

Siamese

Legend has it that Siamese cats are sacred and used to guard Buddhist temples in Thailand where it was considered a great honour to be given one. Their distinctive short, fine, close-lying coat sheds little and is mainly pale in colour with darker paws, tail, face and ears. They also have striking blue eyes.

Expect long conversations with your Siamese as they're known for being vocal! They relish attention and prefer not to be left alone during the day, so shower them with affection and they'll be happy. Full of energy and intelligence, a Siamese loves to play games and can even be taught to retrieve toys.

Burmese

With a light-coloured, glossy coat and wide-set yellow or golden eyes, the Burmese is a medium-sized, long-living breed that often reaches the ripe old age of 20. Spirited and intelligent, a Burmese can be taught to fetch toys and will love playing games with the family. They enjoy being the main attraction and prefer not to be left alone for long periods of time.

Wonderful companions, they're gentle with children and will even befriend other cats or dogs in the house. Expect some noise as they tend to be quite vocal, but they're fantastic lap-warmers and love nothing more than being cuddled – a trait that earned them the nickname of 'cat dog'.

3 INGREDIENT TUNA SCONES

MAKES 24

DID YOU KNOW? That the purr of a cat serves more than one purpose? If, like me, you are under the impression that cats only purr when happy or content, you're missing out on how multifaceted a purr truly is. A cat will purr during labour to self-soothe and also for pain control as endorphins are released when they purr.

Kittens are born blind and deaf but they feel the mother's vibrating purr, it leads them to her body for nursing and critical warmth. Kittens can purr when they're just 2 days old and that starts the communication between litter mates and Mum. Cats purr for a variety of reasons, and not all of them mean contentment.

1 egg	Preheat oven 180°C.
220g can tuna in springwater (undrained)	Line a baking tray with baking paper.
	In a large bowl, crack and whisk the egg.
2 cups wholemeal self-raising flour	Add the tuna and self-raising flour.

Preheat oven 180°C.

Line a baking tray with baking paper.

In a large bowl, crack and whisk the egg.

Add the tuna and self-raising flour.

Mix until a dough forms.

If the dough is too dry, add up to ⅓ cup water.

If the dough is too wet, add a little more flour.

Turn out onto a clean, floured surface and roll out to 1cm thickness.

Use a small scone cutter to cut 24 rounds.

Place each round onto the prepared tray.

Bake for 15 to 20 minutes or until lightly golden and crisp.

Cool before serving.

Store in an airtight container for up to 2 weeks.

CAT COOKIES

SERVES 24

EGGS: In this chapter there is an egg in almost every recipe. Eggs are great for cats because they're rich in protein. In fact, many books that promote natural cat diets strongly encourage owners to give their cats eggs. After all, in the wild, cats would occasionally raid the nests of birds looking for eggs.

80g can tuna, in oil

½ cup wholemeal flour

½ cup powdered milk

2 tbsp. rice bran oil
(or you could use cod liver oil)

1 egg, beaten

Preheat oven to 180°C.

Line a baking tray with baking paper.

In large bowl, mash the tuna.

Add the flour and powdered milk and mix to combine.

Stir in ¼ cup of water, the oil and egg.

Using a teaspoon, dollop the mixture onto the tray.

Bake for 15 to 18 minutes.

Cool completely.

Store in an airtight container in refrigerator, or freeze and defrost as required.

CHICKEN DELIGHT

SERVES 2

GREENS: Although known as obligate carnivores, sometimes adding a few finely chopped, steamed greens to their favourite meat dishes sees our feline friends enjoy it just as much. Good vegetables to offer your cat are carrots, peas, corn, broccoli florets, green beans, zucchini, lettuce, spinach and catnip.

2 eggs, beaten

100g cooked chicken breast, diced

2 green beans, thinly sliced

1 tsp. fish sauce

In a non-stick frying pan, scramble the eggs, 2 minutes or until cooked.

Toss through chicken, beans and fish sauce.

Cook for 2 minutes.

Cool before serving.

CHICKEN STIR-FRY

MAKES 2-3 SERVES

COOKED MEAT: There are mixed opinions about feeding cats cooked meat, but as a treat when you are also making the occasional stir fry for your family, a stir-fry this simple, will not hurt. Another known to excite our little Feline Friends is our simple Bacon & Chicken Stir-Fry: Sauté 1 slice of bacon, chopped and ¼ cup chopped chicken over medium heat for 2 to 3 minutes tossing regularly until lightly cooked. Cool before serving.

100g boneless, skinless chicken breast, finely sliced

50g finely chopped spinach

½ cup cooked brown rice

In a non-stick frying pan, sauté the chicken for 1 to 2 minutes.

Add the spinach and rice and toss to combine.

Remove from heat and allow to cool before serving.

Divide the remaining in half and store in the refrigerator for up to 3 days.

FIFI'S BURGER

SERVES 16

CARNIVORES: Cats don't require fruits and vegetables to balance their nutrition. As mentioned, cats are carnivores, not omnivores, which means that meat is the only type of protein required to fulfil a cat's nutritional needs. However, to feed a litter or any number of cats just meat may become a trifle expensive. Certain greens, eggs and wholegrains help extend meals, for eg., I added the egg to bind and the rice to make these yummy burgers go further, not necessary, but served occasionally, not harmful. You can make these and freeze raw to defrost and cook later.

300g lean beef mince	Combine the ingredients in a bowl and mix well.
1 egg	Shape into 16 mini patties.
¼ cup cooked brown rice	Cook in a non-stick frying pan over a medium heat for 3 to 4 minutes each side or until done.
	Allow to cool before serving.

FISH BALLS

MAKES 12

TINNED FISH: Fish, such as tinned sardines in springwater; tinned tuna and tinned salmon (care with any fish bones) can be offered as a treat occasionally. Generally, cats love tinned fish, in fact some can be addicted to it, as with all things, tinned fish in moderation has its rightful place in a healthy cat's diet. Make a double batch and freeze; not only will your cat thank you, but so will your weekly budget.

100g can tuna in oil

2 tbsp. finely grated bread crumbs

1 egg, beaten

3 tbsp. grated cheese

Preheat your oven to 180°C.

Line a baking tray with baking paper.

Place the ingredients in a bowl and mash into a nice paste.

Using a teaspoon and with damp hands, shape into balls and place on the tray.

Bake for 12 to 15 minutes, or until golden brown.

Cool before serving.

MACKEREL MAGIC

SERVES 2

BALANCED DIET: While cats love all things fishy, it is not advisable to feed them only fish because your kitty won't get a balanced diet from a menu that is solely based on fish. Talk to your veterinarian for advice, but as a general guide, feed them a balanced mix of high quality, premium commercial food, natural foods that include fresh, raw meat and occasional homemade treats that are appropriate for the life stage and health status of your cat.

Ingredients	Method
1 fresh mackerel, cleaned and scaled	In a non-stick frying pan, grill the mackerel on both sides for 1 minute. Set aside.
2 slices bacon, chopped	Into the same pan, add the chopped bacon and sauté, 1 to 2 minutes.
1 cup cooked brown rice	Add the rice, toss to combine.
2 tsp. Worcestershire or fish sauce	Drizzle with sauce, remove from heat.
	Cut the mackerel along the stomach and gently open it up.
	Remove the bones, working from head to tail.
	Fill the fish with the rice mixture, close the mackerel and serve.

MEOW MOUSSE

SERVES 4

CATS: Are meat eaters, plain and simple. They have to have protein from meat for a strong heart, good vision and a healthy reproductive system. Cooked beef, chicken, turkey, and lean deli meats are a great way to give them that. Yes, Meow Mousse contains other ingredients, but eaten occasionally such simple recipes are a treat and your purry-friend will love it.

200g chicken liver

1 tbsp. unsalted butter

3 tbsp. cream cheese

1 tbsp. chopped parsley

Dice the chicken liver then combine with the butter in a frying pan over moderate heat.

Sauté until cooked (it turns grey).

Remove from heat and cool slightly.

Place the liver mix, cream cheese and parsley in a blender and blend until smooth (scraping down the sides occasionally).

Using a spatula, scrape the mousse into single portion containers and leave to set in the refrigerator.

This will keep in the refrigerator for up to 3 days.

MEOW-THFULS OF GOODNESS

SERVES 3

OPTIMAL HEALTH: Cats have a better chance at optimal health if they are fed a little bit of everything. A balanced diet of premium commercial food, natural foods and homemade food. Putting a little thought into what you feed your cat can pay big dividends over their lifetime and very possibly help them avoid serious, painful, and costly illnesses. Treat your cat well, because, for sure, if you don't you'll come back as a mouse in your next life!

1 cup cooked, boneless salmon

1 boiled egg

1 tbsp. steamed broccoli

1 tbsp. fish oil

Place all ingredients in a food processor and blend until smooth.

Roll into 3 equal patties.

Freeze or refrigerate until ready to serve.

SARDINE DINNER

SERVES 2

PERIODONTAL: Did you know that 'periodontal disease' is a disease of the tissues that surround and support the teeth? Periodontal is derived from ancient Greek and means 'around the tooth.' It is by far the most common oral condition suffered by cats (and dogs for that matter). Chewing and gnawing on raw meaty bones provides several important health benefits, primarily helping keep their teeth and gums clean and healthy. Although the bones in sardines are quite soft and not a danger to swallow, they are high in calcium which is great for the bones of every living animal.

200g can sardines, drained

2 tbsp. cooked, mashed carrot

1/3 cup cooked rolled oats

Combine all ingredients in a bowl and mash well.

Serve half, the leftovers can be refrigerated in an air-tight container and stored for up to 3 days.

SARDINE SOUP

SERVES 1

R'AWESOME BONES: Suitable raw meaty bones for a cat include raw chicken necks, raw chicken wings and raw chicken drumsticks (your dog too plus raw lamb shanks). Generally 1 to 2 raw meaty bones per week is sufficient. The bone must be large enough so that the cat cannot fit the whole bone in its mouth or swallow the bone whole.

Always supervise cats when they eat raw bones. Avoid large marrow bones, large knuckle bones or bones sawn lengthwise as cats may crack their teeth on these and never feed cooked bones as these may splinter and cause internal damage or become an intestinal obstruction.

½ tsp. butter	In a non-stick frying pan, melt the butter, swirling to coat its base.
100g can sardines, drained	Sauté the sardines over a medium heat, 1 to 2 minutes.
8 rocket leaves	Mash the sardines.
(or 6 nasturtium leaves)	Add ½ cup water and stir as it comes to a boil.
½ tsp. fish sauce	Finely chop the rocket and add to the pan.
	Remove from the heat and allow to cool.
	Add a dash of fish sauce.
	Puree to serve.

TUNA NICOISE

SERVES 2

This is a purrfect meal for your cat.

Tuna is still the primary flavour, but blended together, there is plenty of delicious goodness in every meow-thful!

195g can tuna in spring water

1 small boiled potato, quartered

1 tbsp. chopped parsley

1 boiled egg

⅓ cup chopped spinach

Place all ingredients in a food processor.

Blend to combine.

Serve half immediately and keep the other half in an air-tight container in the fridge for up to 3 days.

CARING FOR CATS

Getting a new kitten is one of the best things in the world. They're cute, soft as down, and as cuddly as, well... kittens!

It's good to get things started off on the right paw, and the food and care you choose can make all the difference in their health, happiness and longevity.

As with all pets the greatest gift you can give them is love, but other than that, here are some basic tips for you and your 'mew' furry companion that I found, well... logical.

DRY or WET FOOD: Many owners find a happy balance between the two. Consult your veterinarian for the best understanding of your breed of cat and its natural diet, but perhaps wet food in the evening and dry in the day?

WATER: Is an extremely important nutrient that contributes to overall health in every living creature. A cat's normal prey contains approximately 70 to 75% water, so it is critical for optimum health to choose a diet for your cat that approximates its natural diet. Cats also like their water fresh and clean, so changing their water daily allows them to quench their thirst whenever they please.

TOYS: Did you know cats can sleep up to 20 hours a day? But when they're not sleeping, eating, or showing off, they are playing. A variety of toys are a great way to hone their hunting skills, stay fit, and not get bored while you're out. Rotating his or her toys is also a good idea, as he or she will enjoy rediscovering an old friend (or foe). Don't think these need to be fancy, a simple twine of string, a feather on the end of a fishing line or a plastic bottle with a couple holes cut in it, then filled with kibble; the more your cat plays with it, the more likely a treat will fall from it.

CAT SCRATCHER: Cats need to scratch to groom their claws. Some do it just for fun or to ruin your furniture and you've probably already witnessed what they can do to toilet paper! I've seen couch-corner cat scratchers, sofa-safe cat scratchers, a cat scratcher that hangs over a door knob and I've even seen someone turn an old car tire into a scratching post ottoman for their two cats. All of these are much better alternatives than... carpet!

LITTER BOX: Cats are very fastidious creatures. They like their litter box to be clean. If it isn't clean, they might start "going" elsewhere. A litter you can easily scoop from is great for quick and easy cleaning on a daily basis. Daily cleaning also means you can keep an eye on your cat's health for early warning signs (e.g. odour changes, faeces change, or blood in urine). It's also a good idea to change the cat litter weekly, removing all the old litter and giving the box a thorough cleaning.

GROOMING: While cats are very clean creatures with saliva containing natural deodorants and cleansing properties, they do need a little help every now and then. A bath once in a while is great if you have a cooperative cat, but the best thing is brushing. It will help remove excess hair, which leads to hairballs for cats. If your particular cat has long hair, then it is essential to keep it tangle free. Brush often, most cats enjoy it.

FLEAS: Apple Cider Vinegar (ACV) is one of the most natural home remedies to get rid of fleas on your cat. To get temporary relief, you can mix apple cider vinegar and water in a ratio of 2:1 ie., 2-parts ACV to 1-part water. Mix well and pour into a spray bottle. NOTE: This mixture does not kill fleas, but it disrupts them, causing them to jump off, so maybe spray outside... down the street and... around the corner (haha!)

VETERINARIAN: Book to see your vet once a year. As with humans, an annual checkup is just practical, it's proactive and will allow your vet to catch any medical conditions or problems in your cat earlier, reducing potential health problems and potentially large bills later on.

Bird Breeds That Make Great Pets

When it comes to choosing a pet bird perfect for your family the best thing to do is to first expand your knowledge about the different bird breeds. This way, you will never have any regrets about your decisions. Canaries are the most famous among all pet birds and are noted for their vibrant colours and vocal abilities. They are considered ideal pets for busy families as that they do not require too much interaction. Similarly, Budgies also have an affectionate personality and a chatty nature and make great pets. Peach-faced lovebirds are playful, active, and gorgeous but must not be left alone in a cage as they are super social and enjoy company. If you are thinking of buying a pet bird for the first time, perhaps visit a reputed store, share your lifestyle and ask questions to ensure you find the perfect pet for your family.

Bird Life Span

You may be surprised that the potential life span of a bird is longer than you'd think. If you bring a budgerigar or canary into your home, you can expect to share their company for approximately 10 to 15 years, a galah or cockatoo can live 80 to 100 years!

A bird's lifespan depends on its gender, level of care, breeding activity and basic safety practices. For the majority of birds that perish early in life, the main culprit is poor nutrition. The importance of a balanced diet for pet birds (all pets) is critical.

What Foods to Feed a Bird

rspca.org.au had this logical explanation when I was researching "what should I feed my pet bird?"

The types and variety of food that are offered to pet birds are usually very limited when compared to the diet of their wild counterparts so it is important to provide a balanced and varied diet in adequate amounts. Consulting an experienced aviculturist and bird veterinarian regarding your bird's nutrition is highly recommended. The food should be offered in such a way as to mimic the feeding habits of the birds in the wild. Some species will gorge early morning and late afternoon whereas others will feed throughout the day.

Bird Feeding Guide

Provide an adequate supply of foods suitable for the species of bird; check with your vet and experienced aviculturist to ensure all foods offered are appropriate and non-toxic.

Provide a varied diet. You should feed your bird a combination of both high quality commercial food and some natural foods. e.g. fresh fruit, vegetables, seeding grasses, native flowers, green foods etc., that are appropriate and safe for the particular bird species.

Food should be fresh and clean, and stored in a way that prevents deterioration or spoilage. Food containers should be checked daily to ensure there is an adequate supply. Feed should be changed regularly, rather than topped up.

Placing a cuttlefish bone (which you can buy at most pet stores) in your bird's cage will provide important trace minerals.

Ensure fresh clean water is available at all times at a temperature and quality that the bird will drink. Water should be changed daily.

Please do not feed your bird avocado, coffee or chocolate as these are highly toxic to birds, among other substances.

How to Minimize Bird Mess

FACT: Our beautiful feathered companions will make a mess at mealtime; it's just how they like to eat. It's completely normal for them to rummage, fling, take a bite, toss, often dropping and tossing without anything seeming to actually be eaten!

If you share your home with a pet bird, containing mess and keeping the cage clean will be a daily battle; I have seen my Nana (canaries and budgies) and parents (budgies and cockatiels) try for years.

Here are some fabulous ideas we received from the 4 Ingredients Facebook page on how to help minimize bird mess – good luck!

1. Upgrade to a cage designed with mess management in mind.

2. Buy a hand-held vacuum cleaner.

3. Line the cage with layers of newspaper, simply remove the top when soiled and a clean layer will be ready to go.

4. Find the right bolt-on perch, some are designed to direct birds to the centre of the cage; with a food cup, toy or an appealing diameter at end of it? Naturally, when your bird is in the centre of the cage, there is less likely to be cage fallout.

5. A homemade bird cage cleaner that is natural and effective: 3 tbsp. baking soda + 2 tbsp. lemon juice + 2 cups water. Mix. Spray. Wipe with a damp cloth. This will help the smell and disinfect without harming your pet.

APPLE GARLAND

MAKES 1

GARLANDS: One of the things we love to do all year round, is help our feathered friends stay nourished and with the bounty of fruit grown in Australia, a simple garland is an easy way to do this. I've seen garlands made from apples, oranges, pears and grapes – the little birds that visit our garden just love them.

4 large apples, of any colour

Preheat oven 120°C.

Line a baking tray with baking paper.

Slice the apples into ½-cm thick rounds
(I didn't peel or core, I used the whole lot).

Bake for 1 hour; remove and turn each slice.

Bake 1 more hour for soft dried apples.

Times vary due to humidity levels, ovens, apple varieties, slice thickness, etc.

Allow to cool completely.

String the apples as long or as short as you like and hang in your nearest tree.

If you have, before you bake dust with a little ground cinnamon and nutmeg and as you string them, add a grape or two between each slice.

BIRDY BREAKY

---

❶ This comment came from Laurie Jackson:
I do a fresh breakfast for my Galah of sweet corn kernels, peas,
chopped capsicum and cucumber and he just loves it!

¼ cup rolled oats

1 tsp. natural peanut butter

¼ cup finely diced apple

Place the oats in a microwave-safe dish, cover with water
and microwave on high for 1 minute.

Remove the bowl, stir until the water is absorbed and the oats are soft
and cooked through.

Add peanut butter and stir until dissolved.

Stir in the apple, cool and serve.

THE BIRD WHO DARES TO FALL IS THE BIRD WHO LEARNS TO FLY.

BUDGIE BALLS

MAKES 24

FLOUR: Birds are absolutely fine with flour; I use a wholemeal flour because it is made from the whole of the wheat grain making it richer in fibre. Essentially, flour is ground grain which is one of the main foods of many of our feathered friends.

½ cup bird seed

½ cup oats

¼ cup. wholemeal flour

1 tbsp. water

¼ cup raw honey

Heat the oven to 180°C.

Line a baking tray with baking paper.

Add the bird seed, flour, and oats to a small bowl and mix well.

Add water and honey and mix to form a dough.

Using a teaspoon, roll into 24 even-sized balls.

Bake for 20 minutes, or until starting to brown slightly.

Cool completely and store in an air-tight container.

These freeze perfectly, remember they are a treat so no more than 1 to 2 balls, twice a week.

HAPPY BIRD-DAY TREATS

MAKES 24

Glorious sweet potatoes are one of nature's almost-perfect foods and the
centrepiece of this simple homemade treat. I've seen budgies, canaries
and peach-faced lovebirds enjoying these morsels of yumminess.

1 medium sweet potato,
peeled and chopped

½ cup raisins

1 mashed banana

½ cup finely diced apple

2 tbsp. desiccated coconut

Preheat oven 180°C.

Place the chopped sweet potato on a baking tray and bake
for 15 to 20 minutes, or until fork-tender.

Cool completely.

Mash the flesh in a mixing bowl.

Add all other ingredients and mix well to combine.

Roll the mixture into small balls and delight your little tweet-heart!

LOVEBIRD HEARTS

MAKES 6

These birdseed ornaments are so easy and they look gorgeous wherever you hang them.
They hold their shape perfectly and only need 4 ingredients!

---

2 tbsp. gelatin
⅔ cup water
2 tbsp. honey
2½ cups birdseed

In a small saucepan add gelatin to water. Stir until dissolved, then over a medium heat, stir constantly until simmering.

Remove, stir the honey and birdseed until well incorporated.

Set aside.

In the meantime, line a baking tray with baking paper, lightly spray the inside of the heart-shaped cookie cutters.

Carefully spoon the birdseed mixture to the top of each cutter, gently pressing the mixture down to compact it.

Set aside, allowing the hearts to dry, 3 or 4 hours.

Gently push them out of the cookie cutters and let them finish drying overnight.

ORANGE BIRD FEEDERS

MAKES 2

FEEDERS: DIY is what we do and no easier way that using those orange skins after juicing, they are sturdy enough to hold seed, the weight of a small bird, and to withstand inclement weather. Similarly, we've seen homemade bird feeders made from egg cartons, empty water bottles, chipped tea cups and saucers and hollowed out pumpkins. There's nothing like a homemade feeder to get birds of a feather flocking together.

---

1 large orange, halved, pulp removed

¾ cup of bird seed of choice

Punch 3 holes into the orange, evenly spaced for stability and close enough to the edge that it doesn't break when threading.

Cut 3 pieces of twine (approximately 30cm in length).

Tie a knot at the end of each, and thread the loose end of each through the holes, pulling gently until the knot nestles against the inside of the orange.

Tie the 3 pieces of twine together at the top, fill with seed and hang for your feathered friends to enjoy.

VEGGIE BITES

MAKES 4

VEGETABLES: Birds can survive for a while on a basic dry seed diet, however they won't thrive and will probably have a shortened life. So, just as we must eat our fruit and veggies for good health so must our birds; ideally as much veggies and fruit as seed. In particular, silver beet, broccoli, carrots including the green tops, apples and oranges are perennial favourites. Just make sure that the food is not sprayed with anything toxic or harmful.

150g baked sweet potato

50g cooked polenta

50g steamed broccoli

50g steamed spinach

Once all the ingredients are cool, place in a bowl and mix together.

Roll into meal-size patties or pack into moulds (we used plastic shot glasses) and freeze.

These take about 30 minutes to defrost.

Alternatively, if you have a family or a 'chatter of birds', wrap the sweet potato in foil and bake until tender.

Split down the middle, mash and serve the polenta, broccoli and spinach stuffed inside.

WILD BIRD FOOD

SERVES 12

Using homemade recipes to make your own wild bird food is quite controversial; some regard it as misguided and even dangerous. A number of surveys found that 38–80% of households spend their hard earned cash on attracting birds to their backyards. Backyard birdwatching is something many love to do, especially the elderly, it's their small connection to nature.

If you do feed wild birds follow some simple guidelines like keeping their feeding areas clean; avoid bread and processed meats and not putting out too much... Think of it as a Tim Tam and a cup of tea!

---

1 cup dried, chopped apples
(dried apples will not go mouldy as fast)

1 cup raisins

1 cup bird seed mix
(add some chopped nuts)

½ cup chopped prunes

In a bowl, mix the ingredients together.

Start by adding small amounts to your feeder, storing the rest in an air-tight container in the refrigerator.

Depending on how many birds it attracts, top up once or twice a week.

Guinea Pigs (also known as Cavies) are social, inquisitive creatures but being prey animals, they are innately skittish and shy. Although they are commonly thought to be easy first pets for children, they do require your time and attention to ensure a long and happy life.

Housing

Provide an enclosure as large as possible (minimum dimensions for one guinea pig is about 1m x 0.5m x 0.25m high). Two guinea pigs will require double this space.

Guinea pigs are very susceptible to heat stress, which can be fatal. Always ensure the area they are kept in is well-ventilated, provides adequate shade and does not become hot. Animals in hutches and cages can die from overheating easily, offer an overturned box for shady 'hiding' places.

What to feed your Guinea Pig

Guinea pigs, like all other pets, require specific nutrients for them to thrive. If you take the time to make sure your guinea pig is fed a healthy diet, it will go a long way towards assuring that they have a happy and healthy life.

Guinea pigs are herbivores that would usually spend many hours a day foraging and grazing on grass in small herds.

Their teeth grow continuously throughout life, so they need a diet high in roughage to encourage chewing. Chewing helps to wear down their teeth and prevent serious dental problems.

For a healthy, balanced diet a Guinea Pig needs:

- A constant supply of HAY! Hay is paramount in providing a balanced diet and encourages chewing for long periods of time which limits the growth of their teeth, it's also necessary fibre for optimum gastrointestinal health.

- Fresh Vegetables: Feed your guinea pig 1 cup of fresh vegetables daily, but make greens the bulk of that, lettuce, spinach and dark leafy greens are a great base. Guinea's also love asparagus, broccoli, cauliflower, celery, carrot tops, cucumbers, bok choy, zucchini, parsley, dandelion, coriander, basil, dill and mint. Vegetables can be fed twice daily, once in the morning and once at night. Not only do vegetables provide an essential source of vitamins and minerals but they also provide your guinea pig with variety in their diet. Some guinea pigs may not be interested in certain types of vegetables. A great way to overcome this is to brush with 100% orange juice before offering.

- Fresh Fruits: Should be given once or twice a week, and limited to 2 tablespoons per

500g of body weight. Do not feed wilted or spoiled food, and remove uneaten fruits and veggies daily. New foods must be introduced slowly to avoid digestive upsets. If you notice loose stools, you are feeding too much and you should cut out the fresh fruits, veggies and pellets, feeding only hay until the stool is formed again. Guinea pigs are like humans, they cannot synthesise Vitamin C (ascorbic acid) from other food substances. They need to get it from fresh leafy greens and Vitamin C rich foods like broccoli, oranges, capsicum, kiwi fruit and parsley.

- Variety is the key to maintaining a happy, healthy guinea pig. A good rule of thumb is to never feed the same food two days running.

- Always ensure that your protein content in your pellets never exceeds the fibre content. A good protein level is 16% crude protein. Fibre must always exceed 20%. Aim for the highest fibre content possible and avoid high carbohydrate, sugary foods as they can cause bad gut bacteria.

- Lastly, clean water is a must, fresh clean water should be provided daily.

What NOT to feed your Guinea Pig

- Avocado

- Cabbage in large amounts (can cause gas)

- Dairy

- Garlic

- Leguminous plants / legumes

- Meat

- Onions of any kind, including leeks and chives

- Potato and potato peels; the starch of potato is stodgy for Guinea Pigs

- Rhubarb Leaves (poisonous)

- Yoghurt

BIRCHER BOWL

SERVES 2

OATS: Guinea pigs can eat oats but be careful in the amount you feed. Too many oats can make your guinea pig full and gassy and of course cause them to gain weight. Our little herbivorous cavies love oats, as with most ingredients, just make sure to feed them in moderation.

---

1 small apple	Chop the fruit into small cubes.
6 grapes	Place in a bowl with rolled oats.
1 kiwifruit, peeled	Stir to combine.
2 tbsp. rolled oats	Serve.
	On the day of the photoshoot, we made this, quickly photographed it, then ate it for morning tea with a dollop of Greek yoghurt; it was really yummy.

GUINEA PIG CANDY

Red capsicums are great for guinea pigs to eat as they contain a high amount of Vitamin C.

The red varieties are also rich in beta carotene which the body converts to Vitamin A, which is important for healthy skin, boosts the immune system, and aids in night blindness. Red capsicum is sweet and contains about 2 teaspoons of natural sugar, making them much more pleasing to the taste buds; not dislike 'candy' to a Guinea Pig.

1 red capsicum

Rinse the capsicum with water.

Cut a 2cm strip from it and remove any seeds.

Offer to the delight of your guinea pig.

HAPPY VEGGIE CAKE

SERVES 8

Honestly your little 'piggy' will love this birthday cake. Guinea pigs love digging into fresh vegetables and this is one big TREAT in their eyes. Remember, their recommended daily intake (RDI) of veggies is 1 cup, so size your Veggie Cake accordingly.

1 small zucchini	To begin, spiralize the zucchini, carrot and apple.
1 small carrot	Then assemble in a pile on a serving plate or board.
1 small apple	At the apex, create a little divot, into which place a sliced round of cucumber.
½ cucumber	Top with leafy kale, then another cucumber round and more leafy kale.
½ kale leaf, stalks removed	

ICICLES

MAKES 12

If your refrigerator makes ice, then your ice-cube tray is probably sitting empty in a draw.
Dust it off, because in warmer weather, these not only make a gorgeous addition to a jug of water
when you are entertaining, but will help keep your beautiful guinea pig hydrated and cool too!
Just thaw slightly before serving (we don't want any chipped or cracked teeth).

Ingredients	Method
¼ cucumber	First wash the berries and cucumber.
8 raspberries	Then dice into smallish pieces.
4 strawberries	Into the first 3 cubes, place the chopped cucumber.
80g rockmelon	Into the next 3 cubes, the raspberries, then strawberries, finishing with rockmelon.
	Fill with water and freeze.
	These make the most refreshing fruit and veggie coolers or 'icicles' as we've come to know them.
	As mentioned already, just be careful when feeding frozen treats to your guinea pig, defrost them slightly first.

SUPER SMOOTHIE

MAKES 12

When I first made this for Jesse, our beautiful Guinea Pig, I defrosted 2 cubes in a small, shallow bowl. However, the thing with using a bowl for guinea pigs to drink from is that they will very easily step in it, pee in it, excrete in it and anything else they fancy doing in it.

I still use a bowl vs. bottle to feed Jesse water, the boys and I just change it daily, but I found slightly thawing these before offering on a hot day was fine, she gnaws at them easily as the ice melts.

---

1 kale leaf, discard stalk	Place all the ingredients in a blender.
2 medium carrots, chopped	Blend until nice and smooth.
¾ medium cucumber, chopped	Spoon across 12 ice cubes and freeze overnight.
1 medium apple, cored and chopped	Slightly thaw 2 cubes before serving.

VITAMIN C SALAD

A dietary source of Vitamin C is essential for a healthy guinea pig. Like humans, guinea pigs cannot produce Vitamin C, it is an important naturally occurring ingredient and must be supplied from the foods we eat. High Vitamin C foods include capsicums, dark leafy greens, kiwifruit, broccoli, berries, oranges, tomatoes, green peas, parsley and pawpaws.

Kiwifruit
Carrot
Parsley
Spinach
Capsicum
Green beans
Oranges (mandarins)

Simply cut any quantity of the listed Vitamin C rich fruit and veg to make a salad your guinea pig will benefit from in more ways than one.

Keep in mind, the RDI of veggies is 1 cup, and fruit is recommended for a guinea pig only twice a week.

CHICKEN BENEFITS

It touches everyones heart to see a chick hatching no matter how young or old. I recall vividly the faces of my boys in kindergarten watching, eyes wide open, with excitement and awe as baby chicks hatched from their eggs.

Not only are they a lesson about responsibility and love, but also about life-cycles and how in a matter of mere months, those cute little chickens are big, beautiful hens laying eggs for our families and friends.

There are scientific studies showing therapeutic benefits to owning chickens. Already chickens are being used to help those with autism, as well as the elderly. For children on the autism spectrum, it is reported that getting them involved in feeding and caring for chickens promotes independent living skills. They are also said to have a calming effect on children and dementia patients because of their flighty, active natures they are fun to watch.

Chickens may also be a great asset to any small landholding. They control insects and weeds, fertilize orchards, eat kitchen scraps and loosen soil while pecking and scratching.

They provide us with fresh eggs which have a far greater nutritional value. There is more than 7 times the Vitamin A and Beta Carotene (essential for good eyesight) and almost double the Vitamin E in free range eggs. When it comes to the essential fatty acid Omega 3 (which is necessary for heart health, healthy cholesterol levels and positive mental and behavioural health) the free range variety win again with an incredible 292mg, versus 0.033mg in battery eggs. There is also less saturated-fat in free range eggs.

Chickens can also be educational; did you know the term 'pecking order' didn't come out of nowhere? Hens have an ordered social structure based on a hierarchy. If you make room for them in your back garden, you and your family will get to learn all about these rather intelligent creatures up close and personal.

CARING FOR CHICKENS

Caring for Chickens

The trend of keeping backyard chickens has been on the rise in recent years, and it's easy to see why reading the above. However, before you start building your coop, just remember keeping chickens can be cheap, but it isn't free. Like all pets, you'll need to factor in the cost of feeding them, caring for them if they get ill, and possibly even paying someone to look after them when you are on holidays.

Chicken Shelter

– Like all household pets, your chickens will be totally dependent on you for food, shelter and safety. Predators are a serious issue for backyard hens who will require protection from dogs, snakes and the elements.

– As for the size of a coop, the minimum rule of thumb is about 2 to 3 square feet per chicken inside the coop, and 8 to 10 square feet per chicken in an outside run. The coop needs to have a solid floor to keep predators at bay

remember, within a month or two, it is going to be completely covered in chicken poop.

– A full size door is often helpful too this allows you to enter easily without backache as is access to nest boxes from outside the coop for easy egg gathering.

– Chickens love to roost and will do so wherever given the chance. They don't like to too low, so create roosting poles and nesting boxes off the ground.

Chicken Food

A chicken's diet is a beautiful balancing act between vitamins, minerals, carbohydrates and protein. Feeding your chickens the correct types of food, with clean water daily, is essential if they are to stay happy, healthy and laying lots of lovely eggs.

A good quality poultry pellet should be the mainstay of their diet. Grain such as wheat and corn is also good to scatter around.

Chickens **LOVE LEFTOVERS.** They will quite happily eat all sorts of leftovers, such as fruit and vegetables including rinds from both rock and watermelons, sandwiches, cereal, pasta and bread. Some chicken keepers make a mash (warm mashes for cold weather and cold mashes for warmer weather) which is basically a mix of food that comprises anything you don't want to eat, but don't want to waste.

Chickens are omnivores; so don't be afraid to give them meat occasionally. Mealworms, my-oh-my, how they love those and cat food too is a favourite. Tasty fish like tuna and sardines will drive your chickens wild as their bodies crave the high protein and Omega 3 that fish possess in abundance. Protein rich foods are particularly good to help with feather regrowth during a moult.

A well-known estimate of what you should feed your chickens is around 125 to 150g of feed per chicken per day. Naturally, every chicken differs, so if you are unsure check with your veterinarian or experienced chicken owner. What we do know for sure, is that your chickens will be healthier and lay better if their bodies aren't stressed by undernourishment and nutritional deficiencies.

CHICKEN SCRAMBLE

SERVES 6

Yes, scrambling eggs for chickens sounds strange, but believe me your girls will love you for it, especially if you have excess eggs. Eggs, not surprisingly, are a very rich source of protein that will rapidly assist your girls form new feathers during a moult. Also fresh pumpkin seeds are one of the best scraps you can give your girls.

They too are a dense source of protein, as well as being rich in anti-oxidants, so the next time you're carving up a pumpkin, make sure you save the seeds for the coop.

4 eggs	In a small bowl, whisk the eggs and milk together.
2 tbsp. milk	Add the pumpkin seeds and parsley and mix well.
1 tbsp. pumpkin seeds	Pour the mixture into a non-stick frying pan over medium heat.
1 tsp. chopped parsley	Immediately reduce the heat to medium low.
	As the eggs begin to set, gently move the spatula across the base, bottom and sides of the pan to form large, soft curds.
	Cook the eggs until no visible egg liquid remains.
	Cool slightly before serving.

CORNSICLES

SERVES 12

This idea is a very small act of kindness towards your chickens. Not only loaded with vitamins and minerals, but on hot summer days something this simple means the world to your chickens. They will happily peck away at a naturally sweet ice-block to finally be rewarded with a cold corn kernel; and it's a great way to keep them cool and hydrated.

125g can corn kernels (undrained)
2 tbsp. chopped/torn parsley

Evenly divide the corn and its juice across the cups of a 12 mini-muffin tray.

Sprinkle with parsley.

Top with water.

Freeze for at least 4 hours or overnight.

Turn out when ready to serve.

FROZEN FRUITS

Frozen fruits are a fabulous treat that most chickens love, especially in warm weather. Jordana Mills, who is part of our ❶ family said "I've given my Silkies frozen blueberries on really warm days to keep them hydrated and happy. My neighbours give their chickens frozen fruits, she says it encourages them to stay in the shade while also providing nutrients that they love and need."

But as Sharon Wela pointed out "Yes they love blueberries, but remember what goes in, must come out... Don't be surprised! LOL.

PARFAIT

Just as we humans enjoy the health benefits of a fruit and yoghurt parfait. Guess what? So do chickens. They are able to eat many fruits, veggies and dairy without facing adverse effects. Happy hens will result when you serve a mixture of chopped fruits and vegetables with a dollop of yoghurt or cottage cheese.

It's healthy for them too, providing necessary vitamins and calcium which is key to strong egg development.

WATERMELON

Chickens love fruit especially watermelon. Each bite of watermelon contains about 92% water and 6% sugar and is considered a very healthy snack. Its high water content also helps keep our chickens hydrated in warmer weather.

❶ James Malone told us "I have noticed that anytime I put a watermelon in the chicken yard, my birds go bananas for it too. So keep these fruits in mind as chicken treats when planting your garden. It seems everyone loves watermelons!"

THE LEFTOVERS BUFFET

OK so this is served up on a silver platter, but honestly at the end of the photshoot for this cookbook, we simply gathered all the bits left over and voilà – The Leftovers Buffet – was born!

Whatever your chickens won't eat they'll simply grind it around and turn it into a wonderful compost, especially egg shells. For chickens that are laying large numbers of eggs, an easy and high calcium supplement is dried egg shell finely broken or ground and added to their normal feed. Egg shells are actually a treat; would you believe chickens love the calcium they get from them. **Calcium** is very important in a chicken's diet for egg production and strong egg shells.

Offer your chickens a buffet of leftovers, including some of their favourites – cooked rice, zucchini, apple skins, kale, carrot skins, cucumber ends, finely crushed egg shells, watermelon, soggy strawberries, leftover chicken (believe it or not, leftover chicken will be the first thing they pick out – perhaps tell little Ethel it's fish!!!?!) all garnished with parsley.

So almost any fresh fruits and vegetables that you feed your family for good health will bring good health to your chickens and their beautiful eggs too.

NOT SAFE FOR CHICKENS

God bless our little chickens, they tend to get bits-of, leftovers and things that have lurked in the base of our crispers or fruit bowls a little longer than they should have and gobble it all up with pure delight.

Chickens will eat almost anything, but there are foods not safe for chickens; the following is a list of the most common responses we had when we asked "What don't you feed your chickens?" on our Facebook page.

- Apple seeds
- Anything mouldy; of course some moulds are good, but others, including the mould which grows on soft fruits, produce toxins and it's not possible to judge which moulds are good and which are toxic.
- Avocado skin or pit, some say to avoid avocados in general, but avocado flesh is okay in moderation
- Chocolate
- Citrus
- Dried or raw beans
- Dried rice
- Green potatoes or green tomatoes
- Lawn mowing clippings (as they can go mouldy quickly)
- Onions
- Raw eggs
- Rhubarb
- Salt (in excess)
- Tight Squeezes, just nice gently supervised squeezes are best.

DID YOU KNOW?

CHICKENS HAVE A GREAT MEMORY AND CAN DIFFERENTIATE BETWEEN OVER 100 HUMAN OR ANIMAL FACES? THEY LOVE TO PLAY, THEY DREAM, THEY MOURN FOR EACH OTHER AND THEY FEEL PAIN AND DISTRESS (FOR WHICH I'VE BEEN TOLD PETUNIAS ARE A GREAT CALMER). THEY ALSO MAKE GREAT MOTHERS, TALKING TO THEIR CHICKS WHILE STILL IN THE EGG AND TURNING THE EGGS ABOUT 50 TIMES A DAY WHICH KEEPS THE YOLK FROM STICKING TO THE SIDE OF THE SHELL.

CARING FOR GOLDFISH

Goldfish make remarkable pets. Having an aquarium is a great de-stressor and has been scientifically proven to help reduce anxiety (it's TRUE!) Watching your pet goldfish gliding smoothly through the water in a beautiful and intricate dance with the other fish is definitely enjoyable after a long day.

Fish Food

By nature, goldfish are foragers, they have only one goal in life: EAT – and eat as much as possible. Regulating how much you feed your goldfish and when will ensure a long and healthy life for your little gold friends. As a general rule, feed goldfish **twice daily**; morning and night. In terms of the amount to feed, a good rule is to only feed an amount that the goldfish can consume in **1 minute** or no more than the size of the goldfish's eye!

Goldfish are **omnivores** and eat a wide range of foods.

Commercial Food: Available as flakes, pellets and granules, contain all the nutrients goldfish need and should form the major part of their diets.

Plant Food: Peas, cucumber, lettuce, spinach and other leafy greens are healthy foods for goldfish. However, it's best to cook the vegetables (not lettuce or cucumber) for 1 to 2 minutes in boiling water, allowing them to cool before feeding. Goldfish also like tiny pieces of orange without any pith or membrane.

Live Plants: Goldfish like to eat duckweed (Lemna minor), anacharis, azolla and salvinia.

Animal Food: Pet stores supply live and frozen invertebrates as goldfish food. In so far as live food, goldfish eat fish eggs, bloodworms, mosquito larvae, tubifex worms, daphnia and live and frozen brine shrimp.

Clean Tank

The larger the tank and filter, the better it is for your goldfish. Goldfish need a clean and aerated home, the size of your tank will depend on how large your goldfish will be when they reach adult size and the total number of fish you will keep.

Goldfish don't have a real stomach to store food, so literally their food goes in one end and out the other. Goldfish are heavy feeders and high waste producers and their faeces is another contaminant. Toxins rapidly build up in the water if there's no filter, if the bowl is too small or isn't cleaned regularly.

Weekly partial water changes of 10-25% of the tank water are recommended in conjunction with a gravel clean to remove waste and to help keep your goldfish happy and healthy.

Water quality

Good water quality is essential for any aquarium. Regularly test your water for ammonia, nitrite and nitrate levels to ensure your biological filtration is working, you are maintaining it appropriately and your aquarium is not overstocked or over fed.

According to the RSPCA.org.au, other water parameters to keep an eye on include pH, KH, GH and water temperature.

Correct water parameters:

Ammonia	<0.1ppm
Nitrite	<0.2ppm
Nitrate	<50ppm (<110ppm tolerance)
pH	6.5-7.5 (tolerance range: 5.0-9.0)
KH	70-140 ppm
GH	150ppm
Temperature	20-24°C (tolerance range: 8-30°C

Plant Cover

Healthy plant growth is the key to healthy fish. Real plants absorb waste products from the water and provide environmental enrichment. They also offer cover, which will help prevent stress and facilitate activity. The more cover provided, the more active your goldfish will be, dancing in and out of various aquatic plants.

FISHY FACTS FROM FACEBOOK

These interesting 'fishy-facts' were shared on our Facebook page when we simply asked, "How do you care for your Goldfish?" Please, these are simply suggestions, and ones we found really interesting, you select what you think will best benefit the health and happiness of your gorgeous gold friends.

- If you want goldfish to thrive, toss away the small fish bowl and invest in an aquarium with a filter – TODAY!

- It's important to keep any fish tank out of direct sunlight. It's amazing how fast the sunshine can heat up the water, no matter what the air temperature might be.

- Suffocation is the most common cause of death in goldfish. Small fish bowls cannot supply enough oxygen because of such a small surface area, essentially most goldfish in this environment end up suffocating to death.

- Constipation is another cause of death. Fortunately, this is easy to prevent; once a week, blanch a small piece of spinach in hot water for 1 minute and float it in the fish tank. The fish will nibble on it, helping to keep them "regular."

- Most goldfish owners absolutely love their pets. To show their love, they use food. This can amount to quite a bit more food than the fish actually needs. Remember feed only as much as the goldfish's eye – THAT'S IT!

- Commercial goldfish food provides the vitamins, minerals, fats, carbohydrates and proteins goldfish need and should form the bulk of their diet. But feeding goldfish other foods adds interest and variety to their diets.

- Cheerios, our beloved little red sausages, are also beloved by goldfish. Just break off the tiniest piece to try.

- Weet-Bix, this is probably the most common of all human foods given to goldfish. Don't offer in addition to, but as a replacement meal if you have run out of other options.

- Feeding breadcrumbs in place of pellets or other commercial foods is harmful as bread doesn't contain the nutrients goldfish require.

- Chopped broccoli can make an aquarium water cloudy.

- If you are going away for the weekend, pop a teeny-tiny piece of pumpkin in their aquarium. They will nibble away at it all weekend.

PET EULOGIES

There is no easy way to farewell your family pet.

It can be helpful though, to gather together and say a few words in memory of just how special they were and for each to recall a favourite moment shared. Our family has referred to these words, borrowed from someone or somewhere over the years. They've always been simple enough yet with meaning the children understood.

When tomorrow starts without me,
Don't think we're far apart
For every time you think of me,
I'm right here inside your heart.

"Many people will walk in and out of your life, but only true friends leave footprints in your heart."
~ Eleanor Roosevelt

IN SYMPATHY
Thinking of your beloved pet will hurt for a while, but the memories of the love you shared will, one day, replace the tears with a Smile.

Nothing loved is ever lost.

Don't cry because it's over,
Smile because it happened.

BIBLIOGRAPHY

BOOKS, MAGAZINES & NEWSPAPERS

Dye, Dan. Beckloff, Mark. **Three Dog Bakery Cookbook.** Andrews McMeel Publishing, LLC. Kansas City. 2001.

McCosker, Kim. Bermingham, Rachael. **4 Ingredients 2.** Simon & Schuster Pty Ltd. Suite 19A / Level 1 450 – 476 Miller Street. Cammeray. NSW 2062 Australia. 2008.

The Australian 24 April, 2017. **Australians are spending $12 billion a year on their pet animals.** News Corporation. Surry Hills. 2010 NSW Australia.

WEBSITES & SOCIAL PAGES

Nutrition guidelines for dogs and cats
http://www.ava.com.au/policy/621-nutrition-guidelines-dogs-and-cats

Nutrition Toolkit
http://www.wsava.org/nutrition-toolkit

Your dog's age in human years
https://www.purina.co.uk/dogs/key-life-stages/ageing/your-dogs-age-in-human-years

How much should you be feeding your dogs
http://www.petmd.com/blogs/nutritionnuggets/jcoates/2011/sept/how_much_to_feed_dogs-11643

Adopt A Pet
https://www.rspca.org.au/adopt-pet

Most popular dog breeds in Australia
http://www.dogsnsw.org.au/resources/the-lead-enewsletter/1110-most-popular-dog-breeds-in-australia-revealed.html

Are you feeding your dog the right amount?
http://www.petmd.com/blogs/nutritionnuggets/dr-coates/2015/july/are-you-feeding-your-dog-right-amount-32905

Is fish good for dogs?
http://www.k9magazine.com/is-fish-good-for-dogs/

7 tips on how to keep your dog's coat shiny
http://renegadehealth.com/blog/2013/01/02/7-tips-to-keep-your-dogs-coat-glossy-and-shiny

How much should you be feeding your cat
http://www.burmese.asn.au/kittencare.php

What should I feed my dog?
What should I feed my cat?
What should I feed my bird?
What should I feed my Guinea Pig?
http://kb.rspca.org.au

Australia's 5 top cat breeds
https://www.petbarn.com.au/petspot/cat/adoption-cat/australias-5-top-cat-breeds/

Petbarn Adoption
https://www.petbarn.com.au/services/adoptions

Tips to manage bird mess
https://lafeber.com/pet-birds/tips-manage-pet-birds-mess/

Attracting birds to your garden
http://www.sgaonline.org.au/attracting-birds-to-your-garden/

Basic advice on housing guinea pigs
http://kb.rspca.org.au/Can-you-give-me-some-advice-on-caring-for-my-guinea-pigs_40.html

20 convincing reasons to keep backyard chickens
http://www.naturallivingideas.com/20-convincing-reasons-to-keep-backyard-chickens/

What should chickens absolutely not eat
http://www.raising-happy-chickens.com/what-chickens-should-not-eat.html

Fish Food
https://www.petbarn.com.au/fish/fish-food

How should I keep and care for goldfish
http://kb.rspca.org.au/how-should-i-keep-and-care-for-goldfish_456.html

Pet Eulogies
https://au.pinterest.com/pin/20547742021092035/

How to protect your pet from common causes of sudden death
http://www.petmd.com/dog/general-health/how-protect-your-pet-common-causes-sudden-deathv

INDEX

SEE YA LATER
ALLIGATOR

IN A WHILE
CROCODILE

TAKE CAR
POLAR BEA

BE SWEET
PARAKEET

OUT THE DOOR
DINOSAUR

GIVE A HUG
LADYBUG

BLOW A KISS
GOLDFISH

PET COOKBOOK

EASY EVERYDAY RECIPES FOR HAPPY HEALTHY PETS

Kim McCosker

AUTHOR OF 4 INGREDIENTS
THE INTERNATIONALLY BESTSELLING COOKBOOKS